ANGRY BIRDS™

FRIENDSHIP
BRACELETS

Original idea by Kati Nohynek, Rovio Entertainment Ltd.
Instructions by Susanna Mertsalmi, Novita Oy
Yarns by Novita Oy, www.novita.fi
Tutorial videos on www.youtube.com/novitatube ⟶

Content by Rovio Books: Laura Andersson, Linda Lahdenperä, Ilona Lindh & Nita Ukkonen
Photographs by Minna Kurjenluoma and Rovio Books: Laura Andersson, Aino Greis, Linda Lahdenperä,
Anna Makkonen, Laura Nevanlinna, Jan Schulte-Tigges, Nita Ukkonen & Wensi Zhai

Editing by Juha Kallio
Translation by Owen F. Witesman
Cover design and layout by Terhi Haikonen

ISBN:978-1-58923-871-8
Printed in China

ANGRY BIRDS ™

FRIENDSHIP
BRACELETS

Walter Foster

TABLE OF CONTENTS

BEST FRIENDS FOREVER!

Angry Birds Friendship Bracelets teaches you how to make your own friendship bracelets. The bright colors and creative patterns will give you and your friends hours of easy fun. Of course best friends will make matching bracelets.

Tying bracelets is easy – all you need is some string. Just a few simple knots will let you create amazing, complex designs.

First take the fun personality test to tell you which of the ten Angry Birds characters in the book you're most like. How about your friends? Who is the pink-loving diva Stella? And is someone a little stuck on herself like King Pig or prone to blowing up like Bomb?

The pictures in the book give hints about how to match the bracelets with your clothes and accessories. Everyone can find their own style! A bracelet is also a great gift idea: make your best friends presents they'll never forget!

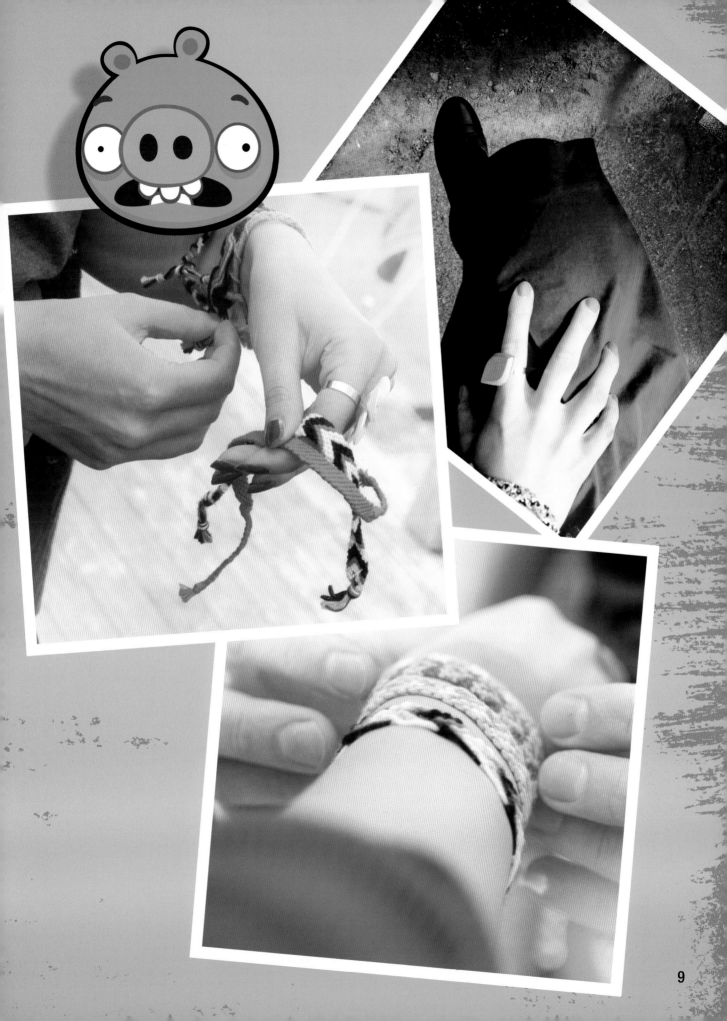

ARE YOU A BIRD OR A PIG?

Before you start making friendship bracelets, take the fun Angry Birds personality test! During the test, you'll get to know ten Angry Birds characters: discover which of them you and your friends are most like.

Read the statements and mark which ones fit you best. After reading all the statements, count up which option got the most checkmarks.

☐ You're a real comedian and you like to entertain your friends.

☐ You have a lot of friends and everyone thinks you're really outgoing.

☐ Your sense of humor isn't always the most sophisticated.

☐ You don't see any sense in worrying about the past and you move on quickly to something new.

☐ If you get angry, everyone around had better look out. Things might start flying through the air.

A:___

☐ You want to make your own decisions. You can't stand getting bossed around.

☐ You have a short temper and you might be a bit of a drama queen sometimes.

☐ You won't admit to being afraid of anything.

☐ You blow your top if you see anyone being treated poorly.

☐ You won't believe anything until you try it yourself. Other people don't always understand how much you can do.

B:___

- [ ] You like taking care of pets and helping friends in trouble.
- [ ] Sometimes you're a bit of a know-it-all.
- [ ] You often find yourself acting as the leader when you're with your friends.
- [ ] You get angry easily and tend to hold a grudge.
- [ ] You will defend your most prized possessions with your life.

C:____

- [ ] You're a carefree type who doesn't bother to get too worked up about anything.
- [ ] You always think the best of everyone.
- [ ] It's easy to make you laugh.
- [ ] If the company is right and feelings are flying high, you can do almost anything.
- [ ] Money isn't important to you, but you don't usually have much anyway.

D:____

- [ ] You are very competitive. You always want to win!
- [ ] You are more sensitive than your friends think.
- [ ] You can't stand to sit in one place for long: you always have to have something new to do.
- [ ] You lose your temper easily, but you're also easy to appease.
- [ ] You want things to happen right now, not in two weeks.

E:____

- [ ] You are basically a sweet person, but when you get angry, no one can help noticing.
- [ ] You enjoy cooking, although you could use more practice at it.
- [ ] You're a flower child and would have wanted to be at Woodstock.
- [ ] Joining a peace protest would be perfectly natural for you.
- [ ] When life gets stressful, you like relaxing in the out-of-doors.

F:____

CONTINUES ON THE NEXT PAGE →

- [ ] You don't like being alone – you want the whole gang to be together.
- [ ] You're always coming up with little pranks to play on your friends.
- [ ] Often you're the youngest one in the group – and you get along with people older than you.
- [ ] You don't always take the time to think through the consequences of your actions and sometimes suffer because of it.
- [ ] You're good at making others laugh and cheering them up.

G: ___

- [ ] People often describe you as cute.
- [ ] Others don't always understand your train of thought.
- [ ] You love candy. Maybe you're even obsessed with it.
- [ ] You spend a lot of time in your own world and don't always concentrate on what's going on around you.
- [ ] You're full of surprises, and your next move is hard to predict.

H: ___

- [ ] You're quiet in a group.
- [ ] Because of your hard outer shell, some people think you're hard to get to know.
- [ ] You tend to eat when you're sad.
- [ ] Almost no one knows about your past.
- [ ] When trouble comes, you often sulk and push others away.

I: ___

- [ ] You have a bad habit of bossing others around.
- [ ] You like showing off your clothes and accessories.
- [ ] You feel lazy a lot of the time. You wish someone else would handle everything for you.
- [ ] Sometimes you act like a brat when you don't get what you want.
- [ ] You like food and wish you had your own personal chef.

J: ___

Record scores for your friends in the chart below and then turn the page to find out which Angry Birds character each person is like! Maybe one of you is quiet like Terence or happy-go-lucky like Bubbles.

	A	B	C	D	E	F	G	H	I	J

Mostly As:
YOU'RE LIKE BOMB!

Bomb is a carefree bird whose most impressive characteristic is his ability to explode on command. He can't always control his power though, so explosions can also happen unexpectedly. The Blues love spending time with Bomb and never get bored.

SEE P. 30-31.

I'M...

ABOUT TO...

EXPLODE...

SERIOUS

HAPPY

ANNOYED

Mostly *B*s:

YOU'RE LIKE STELLA!

Stella is a stubborn bird with a tendency for drama who can't stand being bossed around. She usually doesn't listen to warnings and can get into trouble because of her willfulness. Stella has a strong sense of justice, and she completely loses her cool if someone is treated unfairly.

SEE P. 36–37.

SERIOUS

HAPPY

OUTTA MY WAY PIGGY!

Mostly Cs:

YOU'RE LIKE RED!

Red is the leader of the Angry Birds who will defend the birds' three eggs at any cost. Red loses his temper easily, and it makes him furious when the other birds don't take guarding the eggs seriously enough. At his best, Red can be a skilled leader, but it would be good for him to take things a little easier sometimes.

SEE P. 26–27.

Mostly **D**s:
YOU'RE LIKE A MINION PIG!

Minion pigs are happy ramblers who act on any order from their superiors without question. They always do their best to find eggs for their king. They don't mind not being in charge, because then they have less to worry about. They're satisfied to just be a part of things.

SEE P. 44–45.

DAMAGED

SLEEPY

RELIEVED

Concentration isn't one of Chuck's best qualities. He can be a bit hyperactive. He loves contests and challenges, and doesn't always think about how smart it is to act on every idea that pops into his head. Chuck is good company if he can hold still for long enough. Chuck is faster than the other birds, a fact he enjoys reminding them about.

SEE P. 28-29.

Mostly E s: YOU'RE LIKE CHUCK!

HAPPY

UGH...

YOU TALKIN' TO ME?

Mostly **F**s:

You're Like Matilda!

Matilda is the gentle mother figure of the flock. She loves nature and tries to find peaceful solutions to conflict. That isn't the whole truth though: when Matilda loses her temper, she really flies off the perch. Matilda loves cooking, but the other birds think she still has a long way to go before she'll be the top feathered chef.

SEE P. 32-33.

PEACE LOVING

SERIOUS

OUCH...

Mostly Gs:

You're Like the Blues!

The hatchlings of the flock always fly together. They are happy, energetic birds who like pranks and crazy schemes. Sometimes Jim and Jake and Jay can be a little irresponsible, but they are also very clever and can usually get out of any scrape by working together. Everyone likes the Blues!

See p. 34–35.

COLLIDING

BLINKING

HAPPY

Mostly *H*s:

YOU'RE LIKE BUBBLES!

Bubbles is a cute, happy little bird who remains a bit of a mystery to his friends. Bubbles only talks by chirping, so his ideas are hard to understand. Bubbles loves candy and anything sweet, so you can often find him near the treats. Bubbles' special skill is expanding into an enormous, bouncing ball.

SEE P. 38–39.

Mostly /s:

YOU'RE LIKE TERENCE

Terence is the biggest mystery in the flock, especially because he never says anything. He is big, and his size combined with his admittedly off-putting expression make Terence look a little intimidating. But is he really as scary as he seems – who knows?

SEE P. 40-41.

HAPPY

ANGRY

FURIOUS

BIRD INCOMING!

THE EGGS ARE MINE!

LOST THEM AGAIN

Mostly **J**s:

YOU'RE LIKE KING PIG!

King Pig is the absolute ruler of Piggy Island, whose petty nature doesn't necessarily make him the best king in history. He is childish and conceited, and makes his subjects help him with everything. King Pig's greatest secret is that there are no eggs in his treasure chamber, even though the other pigs think there are.

SEE P. 42–43.

Angry Birds Bracelets

RED

1

2

3

4

5

26

PRACTICAL

PERSISTENT

DEPENDABLE

27

CHUCK

1

2

3

4

5

1   2   3   4   5

FUNNY CAREFREE OUTGOING

1   2   3   4   5

1

2

3

4

5

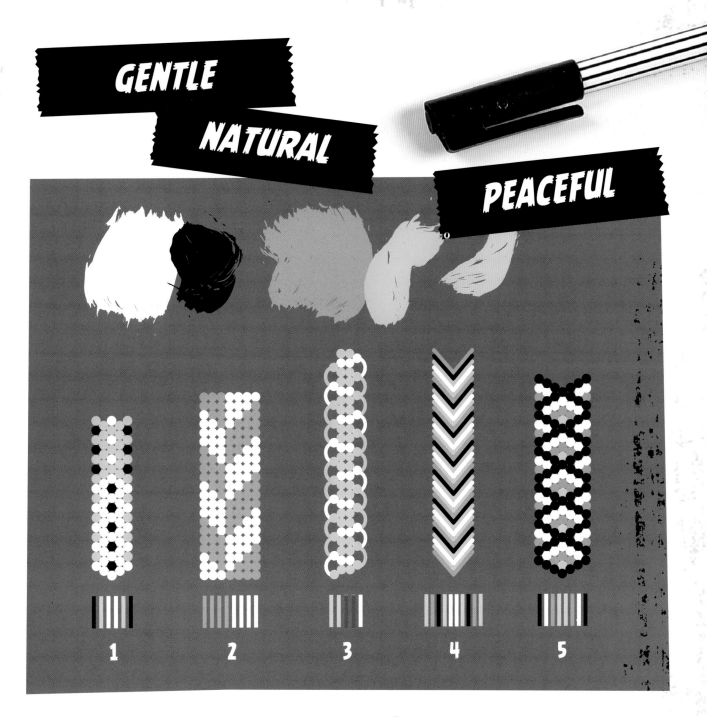

GENTLE

NATURAL

PEACEFUL

1   2   3   4   5

THE BLUES

1

2

3

4

5

HAPPY

CLEVER

SOCIAL

1   2   3   4   5

1 Liquorice, p. 76

2 Candy Stripe, p. 54

3 Leaf, p. 64

4 Arrow, p. 56

5 Candy Stripe, p. 54

1

2

3

4

5

WILLFUL

DRAMATIC

INDEPENDENT

1. Leaf, p. 64
2. Path, p. 62
3. Braid, p. 55
4. Candy Stripe, p. 54
5. Heart, p. 78

BUBBLES

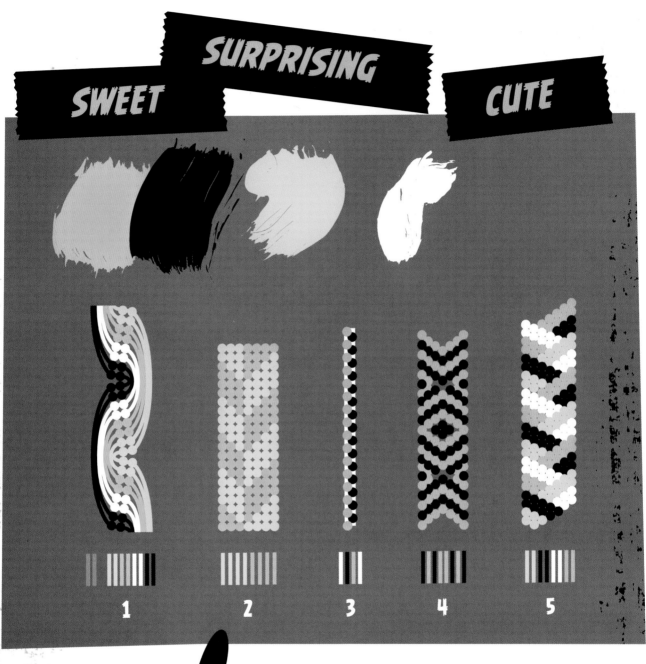

SWEET **SURPRISING** **CUTE**

TERENCE

1

2

3

4

5

MYSTERIOUS

QUIET

BIG

1   **2**   **3**   **4**   **5**

1

2

3

4

5

CHILDLIKE

POSH

EXACTING

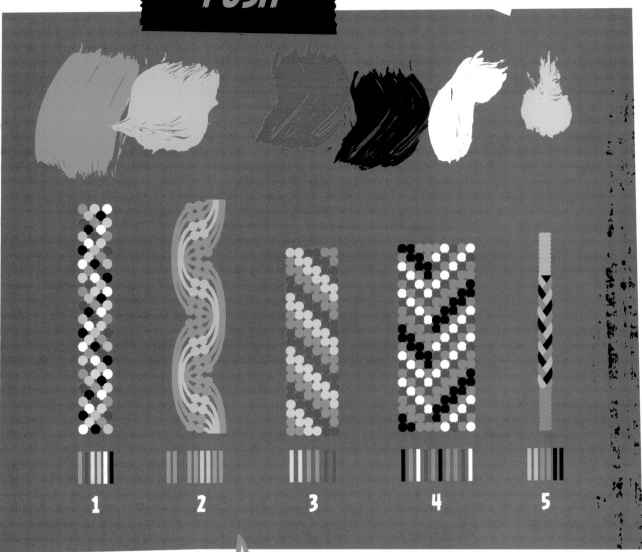

1 Rag Rug, p. 67

2 Wave, p. 72

3 Candy Stripe, p. 54

4 Arrow, p. 56

5 Braid, p. 55

MINION PIG

1
2
3
4
5

RELAXED

GOOD-NATURED

LOYAL

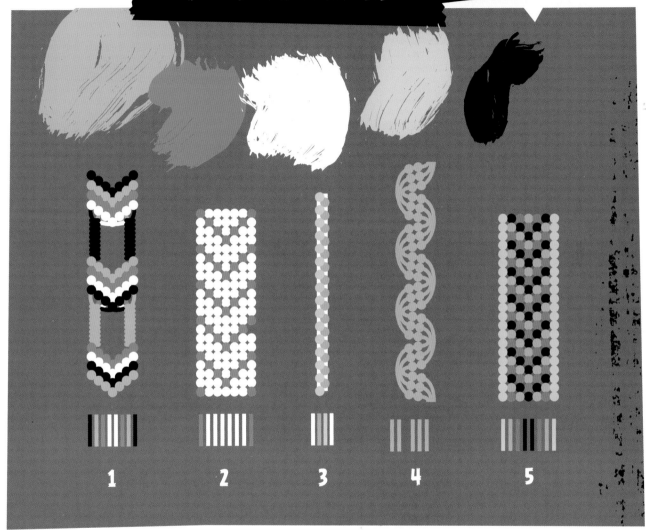

1   2   3   4   5

INSTRUCTIONS

BEFORE YOU START

WHAT YOU NEED

STRING

You can make bracelets out of different kinds of string. The most common string to use is embroidery floss. The most important thing in choosing your string is that it does not stretch. Thinner string makes thinner bracelets, and thicker string makes thicker bracelets. The bracelets in this book were made with super-fine cotton yarns in the Angry Birds colors. Embroidery floss, pearl cotton, crochet thread, and craft thread in Angry Bird colors will produce similar results.

On average you will need about one meter (three feet) of each string. Some patterns use up certain strings quicker than other, so make sure you have enough. Also remember that the wider the bracelet, the more string it will need.

TAPE OR A SAFETY PIN

You can attach your strings securely to a table with tape or use a safety pin on the leg of your jeans.

BASIC KNOTS

You need to learn these four basic knots in order to make all of the friendship bracelets in this book. But even learning the first knot will let you make a simple striped bracelet. More complex bracelets require knowing more knots.

THE FORWARD KNOT
THE BACKWARD KNOT
THE BACKWARD FORWARD KNOT
THE FORWARD BACKWARD KNOT

To learn the knots, first choose two different colors of string. Tie the strings together with an overhand knot and attach them to a smooth surface.

STRING MOVES THROUGH KNOTS FROM LEFT TO RIGHT

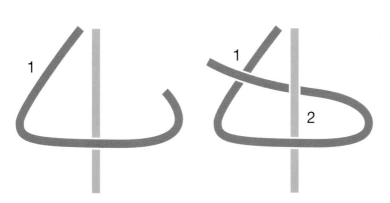

1 Take string 1 and cross over string 2 forming a number "4".

2 Take string 1 and go under string 2 and then up over string 1.

3 Pull string 1 up to tighten. While doing this, hold string 2 tight toward your body.

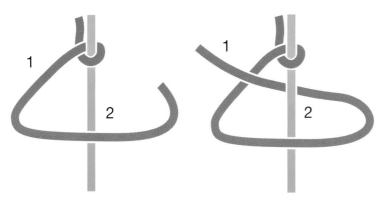
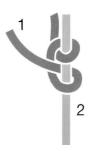

4 Take string 1 and cross over string 2 forming a number "4".

5 Take string 1 and go under string 2 and then up over string 1.

6 Pull string 1 up to tighten. While doing this, hold string 2 tight toward your body. Now your forward knot is complete.

THE BACKWARD KNOT

STRING MOVES THROUGH KNOTS FROM RIGHT TO LEFT

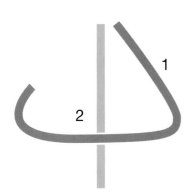

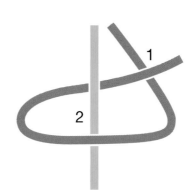

1 Take string 1 and cross over string 2 forming a backwards number "4".

2 Take string 1 and go under string 2 and then up over string 1.

3 Pull string 1 up to tighten. While doing this, hold string 2 tight toward your body.

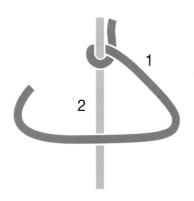

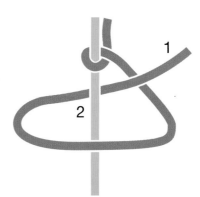

4 Take string 1 and cross over string 2 forming a backwards number "4".

5 Take string 1 and go under string 2 and then up over string 1.

6 Pull string 1 up to tighten. While doing this, hold string 2 tight toward your body. Now your backward knot is complete.

STRING MOVES LEFT THROUGH THE KNOT AND BACK TO THE RIGHT

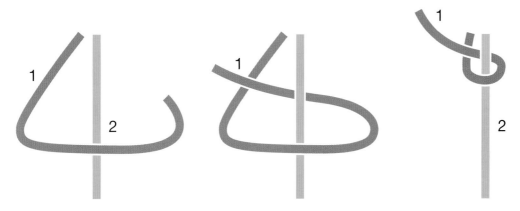

1 Take string 1 and cross over string 2 forming a number "4".

2 Take string 1 and go under string 2 and then up over string 1.

3 Pull string 1 up to tighten. While doing this, hold string 2 tight toward your body.

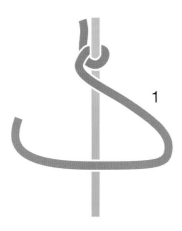

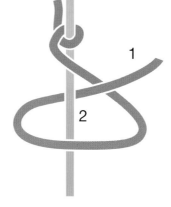

4 Take string 1 and cross over string 2 forming a backwards number "4".

5 Take string 1 and go under string 2 and then up over string 1.

6 Pull string 1 up to tighten. While doing this, hold string 2 tight toward your body. Now your backward forward knot is complete.

THE FORWARD BACKWARD KNOT

STRING MOVES RIGHT THROUGH THE KNOT AND BACK TO THE LEFT

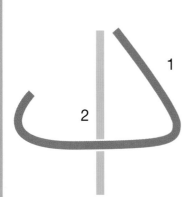

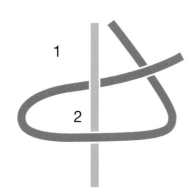

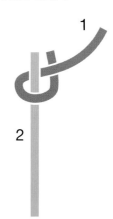

1 Take string 1 and cross over string 2 forming a backwards number "4".

2 Take string 1 and go under string 2 and then up over string 1.

3 Pull string 1 up to tighten. While doing this, hold string 2 tight toward your body.

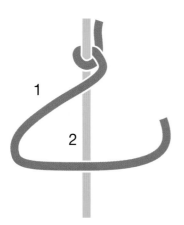

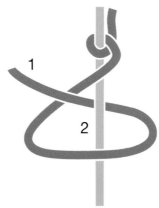

4 Take string 1 and cross over string 2 forming a number "4".

5 Take string 1 and go under string 2 and then up over string 1.

6 Pull string 1 up to tighten. While doing this, hold string 2 tight toward your body. Now your forward backward knot is complete.

HOW TO FINISH

There are lots of ways to finish a friendship bracelet. For example, you can tie them off with an overhand knot or braid them.

You can give the bracelets from the book a fresh look just by changing the order of the colors. You can also attach things like beads or chains to your bracelets. This could be a nice way to use your old jewelry!

CANDY STRIPE

TO MAKE THIS DESIGN, YOU ONLY NEED THE FORWARD KNOT (P. 49).

1 Tie the strings of the pattern you chose together and arrange as shown.

RED
P. 27

CHUCK
P. 29

CHUCK
P. 29

THE BLUES
P. 35

THE BLUES
P. 35

STELLA
P. 37

KING PIG
P. 43

The candy stripe is one of the basic patterns, so it's a good idea to learn it really well.

2 Begin tying on the left edge. Tie the first string to the second string using a forward knot.

3 Continue to the right by tying the second string to the third using a forward knot.

4 Tie the third string to the fourth with a forward knot. NOTE! If you have more strings, continue all the way to the right edge. Once you reach the edge, you have completed the first row of the bracelet.

5 Repeat steps 2–4 until the bracelet is as long as you want. Finish bracelet however you like.

TO MAKE THIS DESIGN, YOU ONLY NEED THE FORWARD KNOT (P. 49).

1 Bundle the strings of the pattern you chose together, but don't tie them.

 **RED** P. 27

 **STELLA** P. 37

 KING PIG P. 43

2 Choose one of the strings and tie it around the bundle in a forward knot. Tie knots to make about one third of the length of the bracelet. NOTE! The knots will rotate to the right around the bracelet.

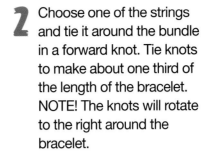

3 Separate strings by color and start braiding. Braid about one third of the length of the bracelet.

BRAID

Fast and easy!

4 When the braid is as long as you want, choose one of the strings again and repeat the forward knots to the end of the bracelet.

55

ARROW

TO MAKE THIS PATTERN, YOU NEED FORWARD KNOTS (P. 49) AND BACKWARD KNOTS (P. 50).

1 Tie the strings of the pattern you chose together and arrange as shown.

RED
P. 27

THE BLUES
P. 35

TERENCE
P. 41

KING PIG
P. 43

MINION PIG
P. 45

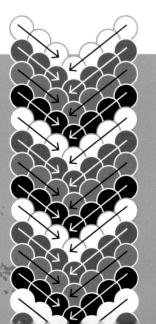

2 Begin tying on the left edge. Tie three forward knots.

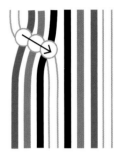

3 Continue tying from the right edge. Tie four backward knots.

4 Repeat steps 2–3 until the bracelet is as long as you want. Finish bracelet however you like. NOTE! If you are making a 10-string bracelet, make four forward knots and five backward knots.

BROKEN ARROW

TO MAKE THIS PATTERN, YOU NEED
FORWARD KNOTS (P. 49) AND
BACKWARD KNOTS (P.50).

1 Tie the strings of the pattern you chose together and arrange as shown.

MATILDA
P. 33

BUBBLES
P. 39

2 Begin tying on the left edge. Tie three forward knots.

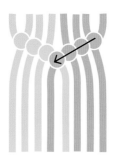

3 Continue tying from the right edge. Tie four backward knots.

4 Repeat steps 2–3 until the bracelet is as long as you want. Finish bracelet however you like.

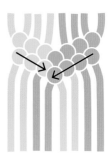

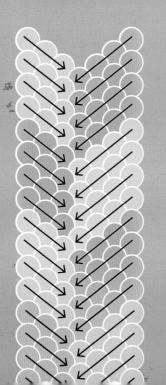

Turn an Arrow into a Broken Arrow by rearranging your colors!

WEAVE

1 Tie the strings of the pattern you chose together and arrange as shown.

**BOMB
P. 31**

**BUBBLES
P. 39**

2 Begin tying on the right edge. Tie five backward knots with the first string.

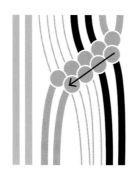

3 Next tie four backward knots with the first string on the right.

4 Tie three backward knots with the first string on the right.

5 Tie two backward knots with the first string on the right

6 Continue tying from the left edge. Tie five forward knots with the first string.

7 Next tie four forward knots with the first string on the left.

8 Tie three forward knots with the first string on the left.

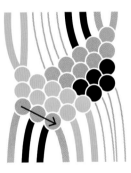

9 Tie two forward knots with the first string on the left.

10 Repeat steps 2–9 until the bracelet is as long as you want. Finish bracelet however you like.

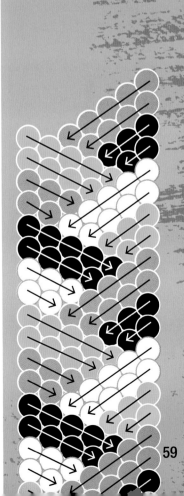

TO MAKE THIS PATTERN, YOU NEED FORWARD KNOTS (P. 49) AND
BACKWARD KNOTS (P. 50).

1 Tie strings together
and arrange as
shown.

CHUCK
P. 29

ZIGZAG

2 Begin tying on the left
edge. Tie seven forward
knots.

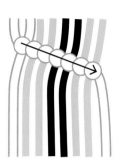

3 Repeat step 2 until you
have made one row with
each string.

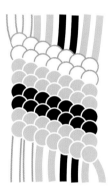

4 Next start tying from the
right edge. Tie seven
backward knots.

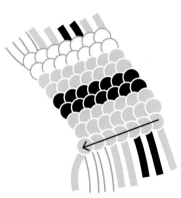

5 Repeat step 4 until you
have made one row with
each string.

6 Repeat steps 2–5 until the
bracelet is as long as you want.
Finish bracelet however you
like.

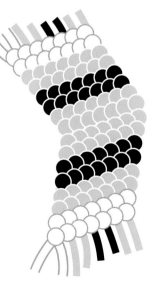

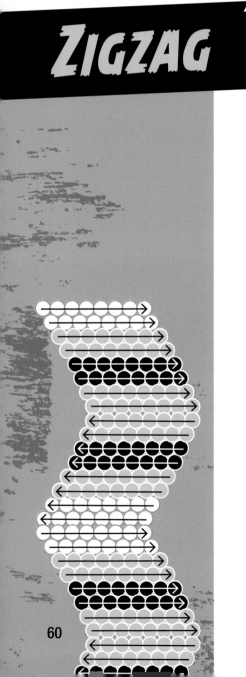

TO MAKE THIS PATTERN, YOU NEED BACKWARD FORWARD KNOTS (P. 51) AND FORWARD BACKWARD KNOTS (P. 52).

CHAIN

1 Tie the strings of the pattern you chose together and arrange as shown.

BUBBLES
P. 39

MINION PIG
P. 45

As you make this bracelet, the string order always stays the same!

2 First bundle the two rightmost strings together.

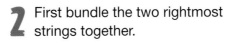

3 Tie the second string from the left around the bundle with a forward backward knot.

4 Next bundle the two leftmost strings together.

5 Tie the second string from the right around the bundle with a backward forward knot.

6 Repeat steps 2–5 until the bracelet is as long as you want. Finish bracelet however you like.

PATH

TO MAKE THIS PATTERN, YOU NEED FORWARD KNOTS (P. 49), BACKWARD KNOTS (P. 50), BACKWARD FORWARD KNOTS (P. 51), AND FORWARD BACKWARD KNOTS (P. 52).

1 Tie the strings of the pattern you chose together and arrange as shown.

STELLA
P. 37

TERENCE
P. 41

MINION PIG
P. 45

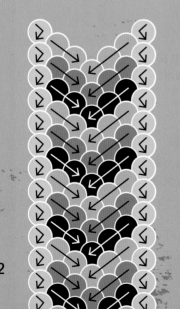

2 Begin tying from the left edge. Tie a forward backward knot with the first string.

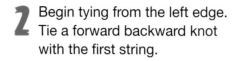

3 Continue with two forward knots with the second string.

4 Continue tying from the right edge. Tie a backward forward knot with the first string.

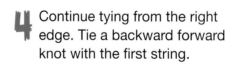

5 Continue with three backward knots with the second string.

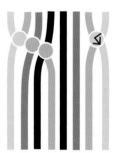

6 Repeat steps 2–5 until the bracelet is as long as you want. Finish bracelet however you like.

TO MAKE THIS PATTERN, YOU NEED
FORWARD KNOTS (P. 49) AND
BACKWARD KNOTS (P. 50).

LACE

1 Tie the strings of the pattern you chose together and arrange as shown.

RED
P. 27

BOMB
P. 31

MATILDA
P. 33

2 Begin tying on the left edge. Tie three forward knots.

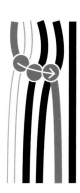

3 Continue tying from the right edge. Tie three backward knots.

4 Repeat steps 2–3 until the bracelet is as long as you want. Finish bracelet however you like.

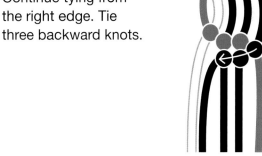

Always leave the last
string untied!

63

LEAF

TO MAKE THIS PATTERN, YOU NEED FORWARD KNOTS (P. 49) AND BACKWARD KNOTS (P. 50).

1 Tie the strings of the pattern you chose together and arrange as shown.

2 Begin by tying the third string from the left in a forward knot.

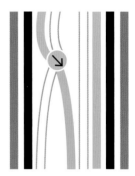

‖‖‖‖‖‖‖	**BOMB** P. 31

‖‖‖‖‖‖‖	**THE BLUES** P. 35

3 Next tie two backward knots with the third string from the right.

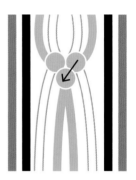

‖‖‖‖‖‖‖	**STELLA** P. 37

4 Tie two forward knots with the second string from the left.

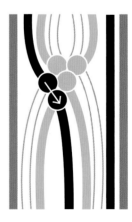

5 Tie three backward knots with the second string from the right.

6 Tie three forward knots with the leftmost string.

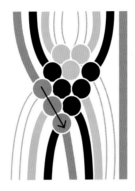

7 Tie four backward knots with the rightmost string.

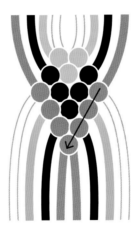

8 Repeat steps 2–7 until the bracelet is as long as you want. Finish bracelet however you like.

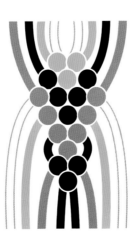

FISHBONE

1 Tie the strings of the pattern you chose together. Separate strings into two even groups as shown.

MATILDA
P. 33

TERENCE
P. 41

2 Bring the left string from the left group to the left edge of the right group.

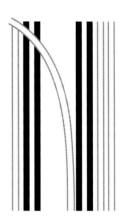

3 Bring the right string from the right group to the right edge of the left group.

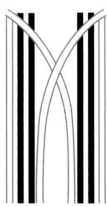

4 Repeat steps 2–3 until the bracelet is as long as you want. Finish bracelet however you like.

TO MAKE THIS PATTERN, YOU NEED FORWARD KNOTS (P. 49) AND BACKWARD KNOTS (P. 50).

1 Tie strings together and arrange as shown.

**KING PIG
P. 43**

2 Begin tying from the left edge. Tie a forward knot with the first string. Next tie a forward knot with the third string. Then tie a forward knot with the fifth string.

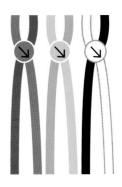

3 Continue tying from the right edge. Tie a backward knot with the second string. Tie a backward knot with the fourth string.

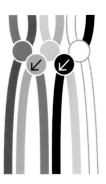

4 Repeat steps 2–3 until the bracelet is as long as you want. Finish bracelet however you like.

RAG RUG

VERTICAL STRIPES

TO MAKE THIS PATTERN, YOU NEED
FORWARD KNOTS (P. 49),
BACKWARD FORWARD KNOTS (P. 51), AND
FORWARD BACKWARD KNOTS (P. 52).

1 Tie strings together and arrange as shown.

BOMB
P. 31

2 Tie a backward forward knot with the second string from the left. Tie a forward backward knot with the third string from the left.

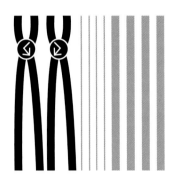

3 Tie a forward backward knot with the second string from the right. Tie a backward forward knot with the third string from the right.

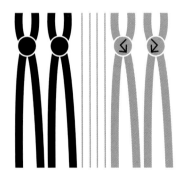

4 Tie one forward knot with the fifth string from the left.

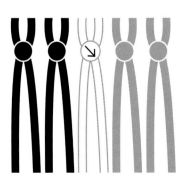

5 Tie a forward knot with the second string from the left. Tie a forward knot with the third string from the right.

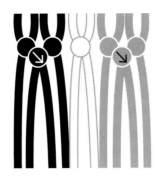

6 Tie a backward forward knot with the fifth string from the left. Tie a forward backward knot with the fifth string from the right.

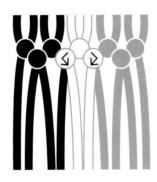

7 Repeat steps 2–6 until the bracelet is as long as you want. Finish bracelet however you like.

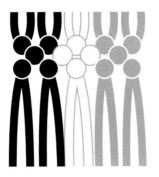

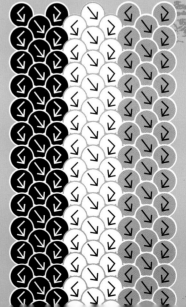

LADDER

TO MAKE THIS PATTERN, YOU NEED
FORWARD KNOTS (P. 49) AND
BACKWARD KNOTS (P. 50).

1 Tie strings together
and arrange as
shown.

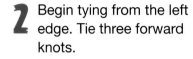

**MINION PIG
P. 45**

2 Begin tying from the left
edge. Tie three forward
knots.

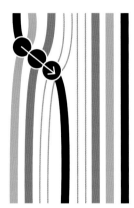

3 Continue tying from
the right edge. Tie four
backward knots.

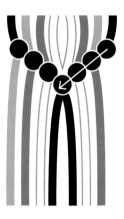

4 Repeat steps 2–3 until
you have made a row with
each color.

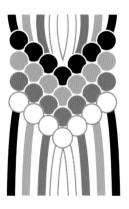

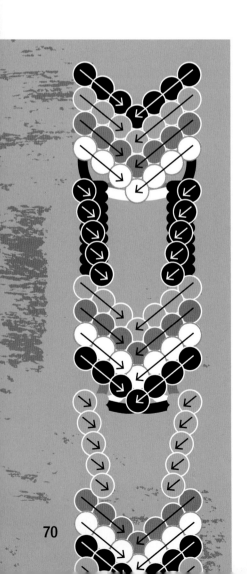

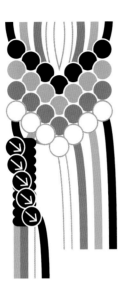

5 Divide strings into two groups. Tie five forward knots around the left group with the first string on the left.

6 Next tie five backward knots around the right group with the first string on the right.

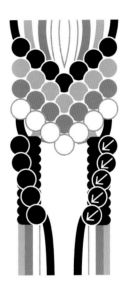

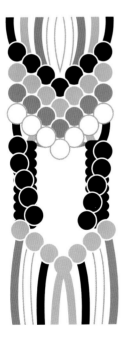

7 Repeat steps 2–6 until the bracelet is as long as you want. Finish bracelet however you like.

WAVE

TO MAKE THIS PATTERN, YOU NEED FORWARD KNOTS (P. 49) AND BACKWARD KNOTS (P. 50).

1 Tie the strings of the pattern you chose together and arrange as shown.

RED
P. 27

CHUCK
P. 29

BUBBLES
P. 39

KING PIG
P. 43

MINION PIG
P. 45

2 Separate the two leftmost strings from the rest.

3 Start tying with the third string from the left. Tie two backward knots.

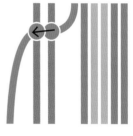

4 Next tie two backward knots with the fourth string.

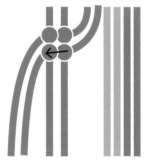

You won't see some of the strings in the finished bracelet because they are hidden by the knots.

5 Continue until you reach the last string on the right.

6 Continue tying with the third string from the right. Tie two forward knots. Repeat until you reach the last string on the left.

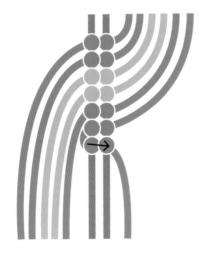

7 Repeat steps 3–6 until the bracelet is as long as you want. Finish bracelet however you like.

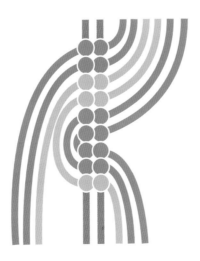

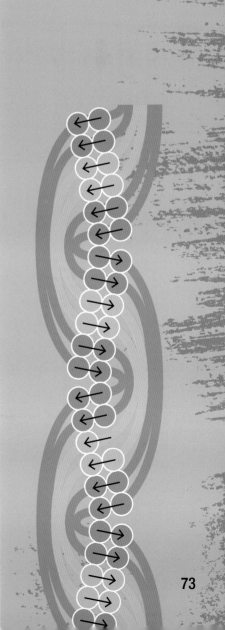

PEARL

TO MAKE THIS PATTERN, YOU NEED FORWARD KNOTS (P. 49) AND BACKWARD KNOTS (P. 50).

1 Tie the strings of the pattern you chose together and arrange as shown.

MATILDA P. 33

TERENCE P. 41

2 Tie three forward knots with the first string on the left. Then tie four backward knots with the first string on the right.

3 Tie two forward knots with the first string on the left. Tie two backward knots with the first string on the right.

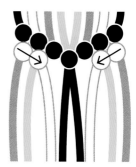

4 Tie a forward knot with the first string on the left. Tie a backward knot with the first string on the right.

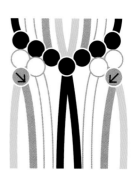

5 Tie three backward knots with the fourth string from the left. Tie three forward knots with the fourth string from the right.

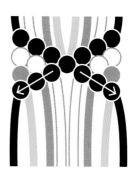

6 Tie three forward knots with the fourth string from the left. Tie two backward knots with the fourth string from the right.

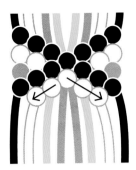

7 Tie two forward knots with the fourth string from the left. Tie a backward knot with the fourth string from the right.

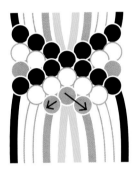

8 Tie one forward knot with the fourth string from the left.

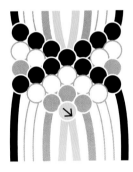

9 Repeat steps 2–8 until the bracelet is as long as you want. Finish bracelet however you like.

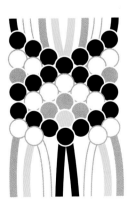

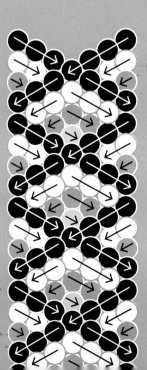

TO MAKE THIS PATTERN, YOU NEED FORWARD KNOTS (P. 49),
BACKWARD KNOTS (P. 50), BACKWARD FORWARD KNOTS (P. 51), AND
FORWARD BACKWARD KNOTS (P. 52).

1 Tie the strings of the pattern you chose together and arrange as shown.

THE BLUES
P. 35

TERENCE
P. 41

2 Tie three forward knots with the third string from the left.

3 Tie two backward knots with the third string from the left.

LIQUORICE

Make sure you have enough string! Especially the two center strings get used up quickly.

4 Tie one forward knot and one forward backward knot with the third string from the left.

5 Tie one backward forward knot with the third string from the left.

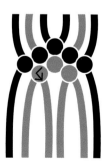

6 Tie one forward knot with the third string from the left.

7 Tie two forward knots with the first string on the left. Tie two backward knots with the first string on the right.

8 Tie one forward backward knot with the first string on the left and one backward forward knot with the first string on the right.

9 Repeat steps 2–8 until the bracelet is as long as you want. Finish bracelet however you like.

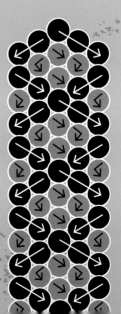

HEART

TO MAKE THIS PATTERN, YOU NEED
FORWARD KNOTS (P. 49),
BACKWARD KNOTS (P. 50),
BACKWARD FORWARD KNOTS (P. 51), AND
FORWARD BACKWARD KNOTS (P. 52).

1 Tie strings together and arrange as shown.

STELLA
P. 37

2 Begin tying from the left edge. Tie three forward knots. Continue tying from the right edge. Tie four backward knots.

3 Tie one forward knot, one forward backward knot, and one backward knot with the first string on the left. Tie one backward knot, one backward forward knot, and one forward knot with the first string on the right.

4 Tie one forward knot with the third string from the left and two backward knots with the third string from the right.

5 Tie two backward knots with the third string from the left. Tie two forward knots with the third string from the right.

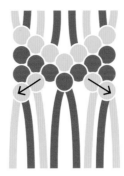

6 Tie one forward knot with the third string from the left and two backward knots with the third string from the right.

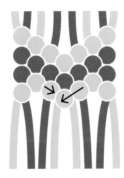

7 Tie two forward knots with the second string from the left. Tie three backward knots with the second string from the right.

8 Repeat steps 2–7 until the bracelet is as long as you want. Finish bracelet however you like.

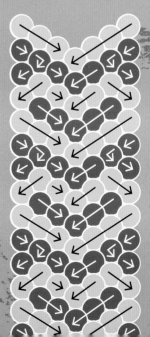

GARLAND

TO MAKE THIS PATTERN, YOU NEED FORWARD KNOTS (P. 49), BACKWARD KNOTS (P. 50), BACKWARD FORWARD KNOTS (P. 51), AND FORWARD BACKWARD KNOTS (P. 52).

1 Tie the strings of the pattern you chose together and arrange as shown.

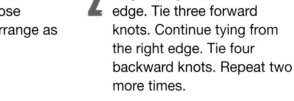

CHUCK
P. 29

BUBBLES
P. 39

2 Begin tying from the left edge. Tie three forward knots. Continue tying from the right edge. Tie four backward knots. Repeat two more times.

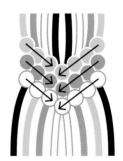

3 Tie two forward knots with the first string on the left. Tie two backward knots with the first string on the right.

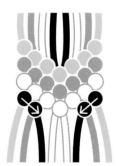

4 Tie a forward backward knot with the first string on the left. Tie a backward forward knot with the first string on the right.

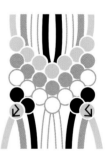

5 Tie two backward knots with the third string from the left. Tie two forward knots with the third string from the right.

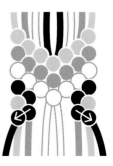

6 Tie three backward knots with the fourth string from the left. Tie three forward knots with the fourth string from the right.

7 Tie four forward knots with the fourth string from the left. Tie three backward knots with the fourth string from the left.

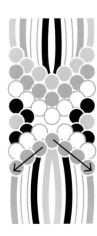

8 Tie four forward knots with the fourth string from the left. Tie three backward knots with the fourth string from the left.

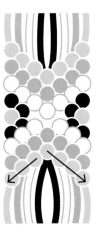

CONTINUES ON THE NEXT PAGE →

9 Tie three forward knots and one forward backward knot with the fourth string from the left. Tie two backward knots and one backward forward knot with the fourth string from the left.

10 Tie one forward knot and one forward backward knot with the fourth string from the left. Tie one backward forward knot and one forward knot with the fourth string from the left.

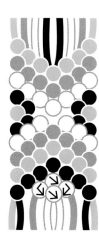

11 Tie two forward knots with the second string from the left. Tie three backward knots with the second string from the right.

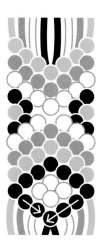

12 Repeat steps 2–11 until the bracelet is as long as you want. Finish bracelet however you like.

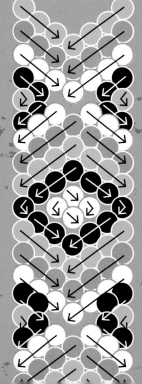

TO MAKE THIS PATTERN, YOU NEED
FORWARD KNOTS (P. 49),
BACKWARD KNOTS (P. 50),
BACKWARD FORWARD KNOTS (P. 51),
AND FORWARD BACKWARD KNOTS (P. 52).

DIAMOND

1 Tie the strings of the pattern you chose together and arrange as shown.

 BOMB P. 31

 MATILDA P. 33

2 Tie one backward knot with the third string from the right.

3 Tie a forward knot with the second string from the left.

4 Tie two backward knots with the second string from the right.

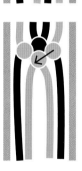

5 Tie one forward backward knot with the first string on the left and one backward forward knot with the first string on the right.

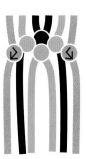

Make sure you have enough string — better too much than too little!

CONTINUES ON THE NEXT PAGE →

6 Tie one backward knot and one backward forward knot with the third string from the left. Tie one forward knot and one forward backward knot with the third string from the right.

7 Repeat steps 2–6 as many times as you want.

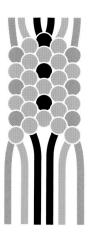

8 When you want to switch the bracelet's color scheme, repeat steps 2–5 as normal. Next tie two backward knots with the third string from the left and two forward knots with the third string from the right. Then tie two backward knots and a backward forward knot with the fourth string from the left. Tie one forward knot and one forward backward knot with the third string from the right.

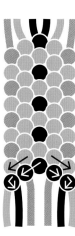

Look at the alternative beginning/ ending for Matilda's bracelet on p. 55.

9 Repeat steps 2–6 as many times as you want.

10 When you want to change the color scheme again, repeat steps 2–4 as normal. Next tie two forward knots with the first string on the left and three backward knots with the first string on the right. Repeat steps 5 and 6 as normal.

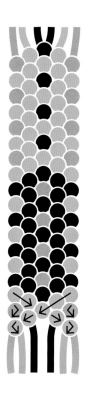

11 Continue until the bracelet is as long as you want. Finish bracelet however you like.

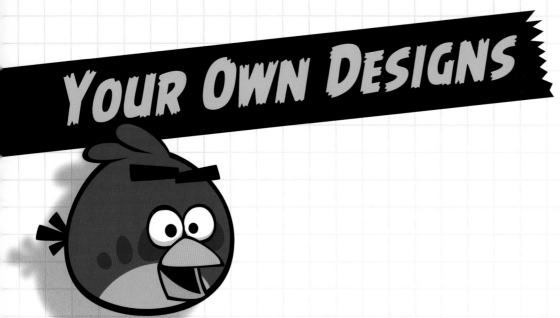

YOUR OWN DESIGNS